D0535897

REMBRANDT

Lives
of the Artists

REMBRANDT

WORLD ALMANAC® LIBRARY

Please visit our web site at:
www.worldalmanaclibrary.com
For a free color catalog describing World Almanac®
Library's list of high-quality books and multimedia
programs, call 1-800-848-2928 (USA) or 1-800-387-3178
(Canada). World Almanac® Library's fax: (414) 332-3567.

Library of Congress Cataloging-in-Publication Data

Mason, Antony.
    Rembrandt / by Antony Mason.
        p. cm. — (Lives of the artists)
    Includes index.
    ISBN 0-8368-5651-1 (lib. bdg.)
    ISBN 0-8368-5656-2 (softcover)
    1. Rembrandt Harmenszoon van Rijn, 1606–1669—Juvenile literature.
2. Artists—Netherlands—Biography—Juvenile literature. I. Rembrandt
Harmenszoon van Rijn, 1606–1669. II. Title. III. Series.
N6953.R4M37   2004
759.9492—dc22
[B]   2004043386

This North American edition first published in 2005 by
World Almanac® Library
330 West Olive Street, Suite 100
Milwaukee, WI 53212 USA

This U.S. edition copyright © 2005 by World Almanac® Library.
Original edition copyright © 2005 McRae Books Srl.

The series "The Lives of the Artists"
was created and produced by McRae Books Srl
Borgo Santa Croce, 8 – Florence (Italy)
info@mcraebooks.com
Publishers: Anne McRae and Marco Nardi

Project Editor: Loredana Agosta
Art History consultant: Roberto Carvalho de Magalhães
Text: Antony Mason
Illustrations: Studio Stalio (Alessandro Cantucci,
Fabiano Fabbrucci, Andrea Morandi)
Graphic Design: Marco Nardi
Picture Research: Loredana Agosta
Layout: Studio Yotto
World Almanac® Library editor: JoAnn Early Macken
World Almanac® Library art direction: Tammy Gruenewald

Acknowledgments
All efforts have been made to obtain and provide compensation for
the copyright to the photos and artworks in this book in accordance
with legal provisions. Persons who may nevertheless still have
claims are requested to contact the copyright owners.
t=top; tl=top left; tc=top center; tr=top right; c=center; cl=center
left; cr= center right; b=bottom; bl=bottom left; bc=bottom center;
br=bottom right

The publishers would like to thank the following archives who have
authorized the reproduction of the works in this book:
Artothek, D-Peissenberg, Munich: 39tr; The Bridgeman Art Library,
London/Farabola Foto, Milano: cover, 5, 6b, 7b, 12b, 13tl, 14cl, 14br,
15tr, 17b, 18bl, 19, 21t, 22b, 23br, 26t, 26cl, 27t, 27b, 31b, 32tr, 32l,
33tr, 35t, 37t, 37bl, 40b, 41tr, 41bl, 42b, 43tl, 43c, 44bc;
Corbis/Contrasto, Milano: 7tl, 10bl, 15br, 31tl, 35cr, 45b; Foto Scala,
Florence: 9cl, 11t, 13b, 18c, 21cl, 21br, 26b, 29cr, 29b, 30bl, 36b, 41cr,
45tr; Photos12, Paris/Grazia Neri,Srl, Milan: 9br

The publishers would like to thank the following museums and
institutions who have authorized the reproduction of the works in
this book:
Photograph © The Israel Museum/David Harris: 9t; The Metropolitan
Museum of Art, Robert Lehman Collection, 1975 (1975.1.794)
Photograph ©1983 The Metropolitan Museum of Art: 16bl; Image ©
2004 Board of Trustees, National Gallery of Art, Washington, D.C.:
28br (Rosenwald Collection), 28bl (Gift of Ladislaus and Beatrix von
Hoffman and Patrons' Permanent Fund); Rijksmuseum, Amsterdam:
11b, 23tl, 24bl, 24–25, 33b, 38–39;

Printed in the China

1 2 3 4 5 6 7 8 9 08 07 06 05 04

cover and opposite: detail, *The Prodigal Son in the Tavern*,
Gemaldegalerie, Dresden
previous page: *Self-Portrait*, Alte Pinakothek, Munich

Table of Contents

Introduction	6
Learning the Trade	8
The Leiden Years	10
Success in Amsterdam	12
Cross-Border Rivalry	14
Religion	16
Marriage	18
Rembrandt's Studio	20
The Night Watch	22
Death and Landscape	26
Etching	28
Home Troubles	30
Depicting the Body	32
Bankruptcy	34
Late Portraits	36
Self-Portraits	40
The Final Years	42
Rembrandt's Legacy	44
Glossary and Index	46–48

Rembrandt's Life (An Overview)

1606 Rembrandt is born in Leiden, the Netherlands, on July 15.

1623–24 He trains in Amsterdam under Pieter Lastman.

1625 Produces his earliest known painting, *The Stoning of St. Stephen*.

c. 1625–31 Runs his own studio in Leiden.

1631 Moves to Amsterdam.

1632 Paints *The Anatomy Lesson of Dr. Tulp*.

1634 Marries Saskia van Uylenburgh.

1639 Buys a house in Sint Anthonisbreestraat (now the Rembrandthuis).

1641 His son Titus is born. Rembrandt paints *The Night Watch*.

1642 Saskia dies. Geertje Dircx is employed as Titus's nurse.

1647 Hendrickje Stoffels begins employment in Rembrandt's house and becomes his lover.

1649 Geertje is evicted.

1654 Hendrickje gives birth to their daughter Cornelia.

1656 Rembrandt files for bankruptcy.

1658 Most of Rembrandt's possessions are auctioned.

1662 Paints *The Syndics of the Drapers' Guild*.

1663 Hendrickje dies.

1668 Titus marries but dies within the year.

1669 Rembrandt dies in Amsterdam on October 4 at age sixty-three.

Introduction

Rembrandt (1606–69) is one of the world's most famous artists, celebrated for his supreme skills in drawing and painting and above all for his ability to convey the inner character in his portraits. He is an artist we instinctively feel we know by virtue of the many self-portraits he made throughout his life. He was hugely successful as a young man, but then he experienced a series of tragedies in his private life. He died impoverished, but as he grew older, his suffering seemed to make his work more daring, honest, and moving.

Painter of Amsterdam's Golden Age

As Rembrandt was growing up, the Netherlands was fast becoming one of the most prosperous countries in Europe. Newly independent from Spain, it was opening trade links around the world, and wealth poured into its burgeoning cities — especially Amsterdam, the trading hub. This created a hungry market for new houses and art and luxury goods to put in them. The Golden Age, which benefited all the social classes, lasted until the late 1650s.

Rembrandt's NETHERLANDS

FRIESLAND

Amsterdam

Leiden

The Hague

SPANISH NETHERLANDS

▲ *A map of the Netherlands, printed in 1648, takes the shape of a lion, the national emblem.*

▶ Artist in his Studio *(c. 1629). Rembrandt painted this self-portrait at age twenty-three.*

▼ Rembrandt Drawing at a Window *(1648), a self-portrait made at age forty-two, is an etching printed from an etched copper plate.*

A Skilled Etcher

Rembrandt was skilled not only as a painter but also as an etcher, drawing on copper plates to produce pictures that could be printed in numerous copies. Rembrandt introduced innovative new techniques in his etching, and his fame spread far and wide through his prints. He was particularly skilled at etched portraits. At the same time, he was an avid collector of prints, and through them, he learned a great deal about foreign artists, such as the Italian Titian (c. 1487–1576). This understanding made up for the fact that Rembrandt did not travel abroad to work and study, unlike the many Dutch artists who trained in Italy.

▼ *This middle-class merchant couple appears in a painting by Dutch artist Pieter de Hooch (1629–84).*

Important Patrons

Rembrandt made his name and his fortune as a young man, painting the portraits of the wealthy rulers of the Netherlands. During the 1630s and 1640s, he was the most fashionable portrait painter in the city. His patrons included Prince Frederick Henry of Orange, the stadholder (head of state) of the Netherlands. He also had important clients among the merchants and professional classes — the middle classes, who were said to be the backbone of the new Dutch nation.

Religious Themes

The middle classes were attracted by small-scale paintings of landscapes, marine scenes, still lifes, and scenes from daily life known as genre paintings. These became major themes in Dutch art during the seventeenth century, and hundreds of thousands of such paintings were produced. Rembrandt, on the other hand, took a slightly different course by specializing in religious subjects. These remained his first love, but they were less fashionable and harder to sell because most people were Protestant and did not appreciate the representation of biblical scenes.

▶ Jacob Blessing the Children of Joseph *(1656) is one of many biblical scenes that Rembrandt painted during his career.*

1606 Rembrandt is born in Leiden.

1609–21 The Twelve Year Truce affords a temporary lull in the Eighty Years' War with Spain.

1613–20 Rembrandt attends Latin School.

1619 He begins his apprenticeship with Jacob Isaacszoon van Swanenburgh in Leiden.

1625 Rembrandt becomes an independent painter. He goes to Amsterdam for six months to train at Pieter Lastman's studio. He paints his earliest dated work, *The Stoning of St. Stephen*.

1626 He produces his first published etching.

Learning the Trade

Rembrandt was the son of a miller, the eighth child in a family of nine children. They lived in a comfortable home; his parents were hard working, modestly well off, and pious. There were no particular signs of artistic leaning in the family. From the age of seven, he went to a local Latin School, where he learned to read and write in Latin and Dutch. He was registered to join the respected University of Leiden at the age of sixteen, but he showed little interest in academic studies. Instead, from the age of fourteen, he studied art with a local painter.

IOANNIS MEVRSI

Academia Lugdunensis

CAP X.

▶ *Leiden was proud of its university, the first in the Netherlands, seen here in a print from 1625. Founded in 1575, it became a center for theological studies as well as medicine and science.*

Son of Harmen from the Rhine

Rembrandt's full name was Rembrandt Harmenszoon van Rijn. It means Rembrandt son (zoon) of Harmen from the Rhine, referring to the Rhine River, which flows through Germany and the Netherlands and past the family's windmill. Rembrandt's father was Harmen Gerritszoon van Rijn. By religion, he was a Calvinist (Protestant) convert. His mother, Cornelia (or "Neeltje") van Suijttbroeck, was a Catholic from a wealthy family of bakers.

Dutch Independence

During the sixteenth century, a large area of northern Europe — now the Netherlands and Belgium — was ruled by Spain. These Spanish domains began to split in two over religion. The seven northern provinces (essentially the modern Netherlands) were mainly Protestant but tolerant of other religions. In the south (Belgium), Catholicism was strictly enforced by the Spanish. A war between the two, called the Eighty Years' War, broke out in 1568 and dragged on until peace was finally established in 1648. The northern provinces, or United Provinces of the Netherlands, led by Prince William of Orange (1533–84), declared independence from Spain in 1581 and became a republic. The southern provinces remained under Spanish dominion and were called the Spanish Netherlands.

◀ *Philip II, the King of Spain (1556–98), was a fanatical Catholic whose repression of the Protestants caused the seven northern provinces to break away.*

Early Apprenticeship

Little is known about Rembrandt's first art teacher, Jacob Isaacszoon van Swanenburgh (1571–1638), except that he was a painter of historical scenes who was well known in Leiden. He was a Catholic and had spent some time in Italy. Very few of his works survive. Nonetheless, he must have given the young Rembrandt a solid grounding in his trade.

▶ *This detail of a painting by Rembrandt's friend Jan Lievens (1607–74) shows a young apprentice artist busy studying.*

Pieter Lastman

The most important spell in Rembrandt's early training came in 1625 when he spent six months in Amsterdam at the studio of Pieter Lastman (1583–1633), one of the most famous artists of the Netherlands at the time. Like van Swanenburgh, Lastman had been to Italy and had adopted the grand, dramatic style associated with Italian art. He applied it to scenes based on history, classical myths, or the Bible, attempting to make them look authentic by including details such as antique clothing — an approach that Rembrandt also adopted.

▼ *Rembrandt's* Balaam's Ass and the Angel *(1626) owed much to Lastman's version.*

▲ Balaam's Ass and the Angel *(1622) by Pieter Lastman. This Old Testament story relates how Balaam beat his donkey because he could not see the angel blocking the way.*

▼ *This* Self-Portrait *(1629) of Rembrandt at about twenty-three shows youthful energy and vigor.*

Rembrandt on His Own

Rembrandt's work after his trip to Amsterdam shows that Lastman had made a deep impression. A number of his paintings from this period are very similar to works by Lastman. Rembrandt clearly wished to be seen as a serious artist who could take on grand scenes. Working from his own studio in Leiden, he was beginning to have some success and to attract public attention as the miller's son with a remarkable talent.

The Leiden Years

1625 Rembrandt works in close association with fellow artist Jan Lievens.

1628 Gerrit Dou becomes one of Rembrandt's first pupils. One of Rembrandt's paintings is bought by an English ambassador and given to King Charles I. Constantijn Huygens visits Rembrandt's studio, paving the way to commissions from the court in The Hague.

1630 Rembrandt's father dies. Another pupil, Isaac de Jouderville, joins Rembrandt's studio.

1631 Rembrandt meets the Amsterdam art dealer Hendrick van Uylenburgh. He enters a business partnership with van Uylenburgh, putting down 1000 guilders (a large sum of money) as a loan.

During the early years of Rembrandt's career in Leiden, the quality of his painting improved vastly, and his highly original artistic vision began to emerge. His work took on a new sophistication with his use of dramatic lighting, following a technique that had been pioneered by the Italian artist Caravaggio. Although still only in his early twenties, Rembrandt quickly achieved fame. Always ambitious, he carefully cultivated contacts with leading citizens of the United Provinces of the Netherlands.

▶ *This detail from a Dutch painting depicts an art collector contemplating a purchase.*

The Art Market

It is estimated that, during the first half of the seventeenth century, some twenty million pieces of art were produced in Amsterdam alone. The thirst for paintings was insatiable; even very modest homes had them. Into this heated market also came major paintings from all over Europe. Rembrandt always claimed that he did not need to travel to Italy because he could see enough Italian art in the Netherlands.

Biblical Scenes

Like Lastman, Rembrandt was particularly fond of painting biblical scenes. This does not seem to have been driven by any deep sense of piety. Rather, Rembrandt was aware that the outstanding figures in the history of art, such as the Italians Titian, Leonardo da Vinci (1452–1519), and Tintoretto (1518–94), had demonstrated their greatness through their religious art. He wanted to rank among them. Yet he also bought to these subjects a new intimacy and charm. A painting like *The Presentation of Jesus in the Temple* shows just how much his work had advanced since *Balaam's Ass and the Angel*, painted barely two years before.

◀ *In* The Presentation of Jesus in the Temple *(1631), Rembrandt makes a dramatic impact with his use of a spotlight effect on the central figures, who are comparatively small in relation to the whole picture.*

Caravaggio

The Italian artist Caravaggio (1571–1610) belonged to the generation before Rembrandt, but his striking use of light and shadow was still the object of fascination for artists and art lovers throughout Europe. Caravaggio was the master of *luminismo* (meaning "luminism" in Italian) — a painting technique based on strong contrasts between light and shadow. He applied this effect to biblical scenes, coupled with a technical skill that made his paintings look almost photographic. Many of the Dutch artists who went to Italy to study at this time returned as committed Caravaggists. The most successful was Gerrit van Honthorst (1590–1656), who earned the nickname "Gerard of the Night Scenes."

▶ The Calling of St. Matthew *(c. 1599) by Caravaggio shows his dramatic use of a single source of strong light.*

▲ Constantijn Huygens and his Clerk *(1627), by the Amsterdam artist Thomas de Keyser (1597–1667).*

Jan Lievens

In these Leiden years, Rembrandt shared his studio with another gifted artist of his own age called Jan Lievens. Lievens had also trained for a short while under Lastman, several years before Rembrandt in 1618–20. The work of Lievens and Rembrandt at this time was remarkably similar — so similar, in fact, that it is hard to tell their paintings apart.

▼ Portrait of Rembrandt *(c. 1628) by Jan Lievens.*

Making Connections

A mark of Rembrandt's success was the visit of Constantijn Huygens (1596–1687) in 1628. Huygens, a scholar and a widely traveled diplomat, was secretary to Prince Frederick Henry of Orange (1584–1647), the stadholder, who held court in The Hague, the administrative capital of the Netherlands. After the visit, Huygens returned to The Hague with glowing praise for both Rembrandt and Lievens. It proved to be a valuable connection; through Huygens, Rembrandt won lucrative commissions from members of the Dutch court and even from Prince Frederick Henry himself. For the miller's son, this represented an immediate boost in status.

1632 Rembrandt moves to Amsterdam. He paints his first commissioned portrait, of Nicholaes Ruts, an Amsterdam merchant. During a trip to The Hague, he paints a portrait of Princess Amalia van Solms, the wife of Prince Frederick Henry. He also completes *The Anatomy Lesson of Dr. Tulp*. Lievens goes to work in England, where he stays for two years.

1633 Pieter Lastman dies. Rembrandt acknowledges his debt to him in a series of drawings.

Success in Amsterdam

Sometime in early 1632, at the age of twenty-five, Rembrandt went to Amsterdam to stay with the art dealer Hendrick van Uylenburgh (1587–1661). Uylenburgh had a gallery as well as an academy for training young artists, which Rembrandt helped to run as a productive studio. Through van Uylenburgh's contacts, Rembrandt soon became one of Amsterdam's most fashionable portrait painters.

Amsterdam

When Rembrandt arrived in Amsterdam, it was at the height of its so-called "Golden Age" — vibrant, wealthy, confident, cosmopolitan, and cultured. A seaport, it was at the heart of a web of trade links that had spanned Europe since the Middle Ages and now reached around the world. With a population of about two hundred thousand, it ranked as the third-largest city in Europe (after Paris and London) and was expanding quickly with a web of new canals lined by mansions.

▲ *A seventeenth-century Dutch drawing shows the variety of coloration and petal shape that could raise the value of tulip species.*

Tulipmania

The new wealth of Amsterdam inspired a get-rich-quick mentality of wild financial speculation. The most spectacular episode was the craze for tulips in the 1630s. Tulips were still comparatively new to the Netherlands, and the Dutch developed a fascination for them. Rare hybrid blooms — and promises on paper for future bulbs — started to change hands at astronomical prices. In 1637, people realized that these were just flowers, and the once-priceless bulbs — and the paper promises — suddenly became worthless. Hundreds of speculators were financially ruined.

The Dutch East India Company

A key to the success of Amsterdam was the presence of Dutch East India Company. It had been founded by a group of Dutch cities in 1602 as a trading association. The voyages to the Far East by the Dutch explorer Cornelis de Houtman (1540–99) in 1595–7 inspired them to speculate that vast profits could be made from the trade in luxury items from the East, such as porcelain, spices, and silk. They proved right: as it spread its network of trading stations and colonies halfway around the world, the Dutch East India Company brought vast wealth to Amsterdam. Shareholders came from all levels of society: they included servants and laborers. A less prominent Dutch West India Company was founded in 1621, dealing mainly in African slaves.

▶ *A wooden sculpture from India depicts a visiting merchant from the Dutch East India Company.*

▼ *Dam Square, pictured in a painting of 1659, wa — and still is — the bus heart of Amsterdam*

▼ *Rembrandt's Portrait of Maurits Huygens (1632) was probably painted in The Hague. Maurits was the elder brother of Constantijn.*

Portraits of Amsterdam

Within a few months of his arrival, Rembrandt had established himself as one of the leading portrait painters of Amsterdam. Van Uylenburgh had good connections among the higher ranks of Amsterdam society, including the city's regents — the council of forty-eight leading figures in government, law, and trade. It was a lucrative business: in his first two years in the city, Rembrandt painted some fifty portraits. But Rembrandt's character was not entirely suited to this work: he could seem impatient, arrogant, argumentative, and socially awkward, which upset his clients and patrons alike.

▶ *Public anatomical demonstrations took place in De Waag, one of the old city gates of Amsterdam.*

The Anatomy Lesson of Dr. Tulp

A key to Rembrandt's early success in Amsterdam was *The Anatomy Lesson of Dr. Tulp* (1632), a group portrait that gave him an introduction to many of the leading families of the city. The subject was a public anatomy demonstration by the leader of Amsterdam's Guild of Surgeons. Other painters had tackled the subject before; the task for Rembrandt was to inject originality into it.

This he did by creating a remarkable pyramidal composition. Each of the figures is treated as an individual portrait, but because they are all concentrating on the main event — the rather gruesome dissection of a cadaver, from which the light radiates — the picture has a unity that is rare in group portraits.

▼ *In* The Anatomy Lesson of Dr. Tulp *(1632), Rembrandt used Caravaggio-style lighting to bring drama to an ambitious group portrait.*

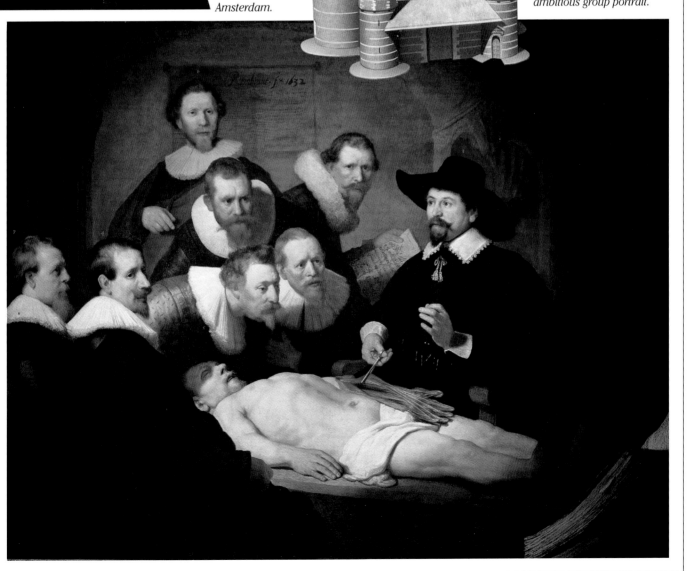

1610–14 Rubens paints the *Raising of the Cross* and *Descent from the Cross* for Antwerp cathedral.

1628–30 Rubens travels first to Spain, then to England, where he helps negotiate a peace settlement, for which he is knighted by King Charles I.

c. 1633 Rembrandt paints his versions of the *Raising of the Cross* and *Descent from the Cross*.

1635 Rembrandt paints *The Abduction of Ganymede*.

1639 Rembrandt sketches Raphael's *Portrait of Baldassare Castiglione* at a sale but fails to buy it.

1640 Rubens dies.

Cross-Border Rivalry

▼ *Coins bore the head of Rubens' patron, Philip IV, King of Spain (1621–65).*

Rembrandt believed he had talent to rival the greatest painters of his day, even the leading artist of neighboring Spanish Netherlands, a Flemish painter celebrated throughout Europe, Peter Paul Rubens (1577–1640). Rembrandt knew that Rubens, almost thirty years his senior, was nearing the end of his career. Although both were talented artists, they had different gifts.

◀ The Judgment of Paris *(1639) is typical of Rubens' work, full of dynamic movement and a spirit of luxurious sensuality.*

The Genius of Rubens

When Rembrandt was two years old, Rubens returned from Italy to his home city of Antwerp after an eight-year visit. Already a gifted artist, he had discovered a new vigor and panache in Italy, and he combined exceptional technical skills with a dynamic sense of composition. He became court painter to Archduke Albert and Infanta Isabella (daughter of Philip II), who ruled over the Spanish Netherlands on behalf of Spain. In 1610–14, he demonstrated his exceptional talents in a pair of triptychs for Antwerp cathedral. Thereafter, commissions poured in, which he met by using a team of assistants.

Rubens, Spanish Envoy

Rubens' work caught the imagination of the ruling elites of Europe, and it rang with the new self-confidence of the Catholic Counter-Reformation. His talent and standing in the art world qualified Rubens as an ambassador for the Infanta Isabella, and he traveled widely, working for the royal families of England, France, and Spain.

▶ *Rubens painted this* Self-Portrait *(1639) when he was about sixty years old.*

Titian's Legacy

An inspiration to both Rubens and Rembrandt was the Italian painter Titian, the greatest painter to emerge from Venice. Using his masterly technique and distinctive clarity of color, Titian created scenes from the Bible, classical mythology, and history that were full of energy and verve. On the other hand, his portraits combine a powerful sense of realism, immediacy, and human sympathy that particularly appealed to Rembrandt.

▶ *Rembrandt's* The Abduction of Ganymede *(1635) depicts the moment when the infant Trojan is carried off by the eagle of Zeus to become cupbearer to the gods.*

Rembrandt's Myths

Rembrandt understood that paintings of myths and biblical scenes were a route to international recognition. During the 1630s, he did a series of paintings on classical mythology. Rubens may have been an inspiration, but Rembrandt's classical myths are always subtly different. In Rembrandt's work, the impact is always less heroic and grandiose; his figures are more humble. Perhaps as a response to the down-to-earth humanism of Dutch Protestantism, Rembrandt's tendency was to portray myth as an extension of ordinary life.

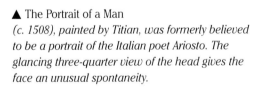

▲ The Portrait of a Man
(c. 1508), painted by Titian, was formerly believed to be a portrait of the Italian poet Ariosto. The glancing three-quarter view of the head gives the face an unusual spontaneity.

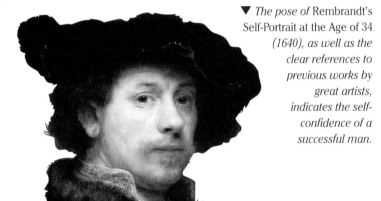

▼ *The pose of* Rembrandt's Self-Portrait at the Age of 34 *(1640), as well as the clear references to previous works by great artists, indicates the self-confidence of a successful man.*

An Inspired Portrait

Rembrandt studied the work of the great artists of the past and was happy to refer to them in his own paintings. The posture of his *Self-Portrait at the Age of 34* is clearly modeled on Titian's *Portrait of a Man*. The antiquated clothing bears strong resemblance to the *Portrait of Baldassare Castiglione* (c. 1516), by the Italian artist Raphael (1483–1520). Rembrandt had seen both the Titian and the Raphael when they were in the possession of a merchant in Amsterdam called Alfonso Lopez.

Religion

1530s Protestant ideas reach the Netherlands, including Calvinism, named after its Swiss founder John Calvin (1509–64).

1565 Extreme Protestants begin a campaign of destruction, called iconoclasm, that strips churches of their ornaments and destroys much of the Netherlands' medieval artistic heritage.

1579 The Union of Utrecht upholds the freedom of religious belief in the seven Dutch provinces. The Calvinists take control of government. They begin whitewashing the interiors of churches.

Religion played a central role in Dutch life in the seventeenth century. It was the cause of wars, the defining feature of political factions, and at the center of intellectual debate. Many artists responded by avoiding religious subject matter altogether. Not so Rembrandt — indeed, biblical painting remained at the center of his art throughout his artistic career.

Religion in the Netherlands

The Dutch Republic (United Provinces of the Netherlands) was founded on a belief in religious tolerance. Protestants ruled, but there were many competing factions among them, such as the Calvinists (and the Dutch Reformed Church), the Remonstrants, and the Mennonites. Catholics were tolerated, although they were not permitted to worship publicly. Hendrick van Uylenburgh was a Mennonite, a member of a strict religious sect. Through him, Rembrandt came to know and paint a number of leading figures in Amsterdam's religious community.

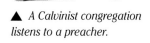

▲ *A Calvinist congregation listens to a preacher.*

Prints and Engravings

Much of Rembrandt's information about the religious painting of other artists came through the thousands of prints that were in circulation. Rembrandt himself had a large collection. Prints of famous paintings were made by specialist studios, and living artists also made prints of their own works. However, black and white prints could only give indirect knowledge of works of art, limited to composition and content.

▶ *Rembrandt's drawing,* The Last Supper *(c. 1635), echoes the fresco* The Last Supper *(c. 1495–7) by Leonardo da Vinci, which Rembrandt could only have seen in a print.*

▼ *The Dutch artist Michiel Mierevelt (1567–1641) painted this portrait of Prince Frederick Henry in about 1632.*

Prince Frederick Henry

Through the offices of Constantijn Huygens, Rembrandt received important commissions for religious work from Prince Frederick Henry. It seems, however, that during the late 1630s, the relationship between Rembrandt and Prince Frederick Henry cooled over wrangles about payment for further paintings.

Rembrandt's Biblical Works

From early training under Pieter Lastman, Rembrandt often chose to depict unusual biblical scenes, such as Belshazzar's feast. They could be interpreted as teaching moral lessons. In the case of *The Feast of Belshazzar*, the subject suggested the vanity of riches in the presence of plague, which visited the Netherlands in the mid-1630s. At this stage in his career, Rembrandt was drawn primarily to intense and dramatic scenes from the Old Testament and the Passion of Christ — the events surrounding his crucifixion. Later, Rembrandt turned to more tender and compassionate themes from Christ's mission.

▶ *In the 1670s, the Portuguese (right) and Ashkenazic synagogues were built opposite each other in the Jewish quarter of Amsterdam, close to the city center.*

▼ *In* The Feast of Belshazzar *(1635), Rembrandt depicts the famous biblical scene from the* Book of Daniel *in which the destruction of Babylon is foretold by the mysterious writing on the wall.*

The Jewish Community in Amsterdam

Religious tolerance in Amsterdam extended to the Jewish community. In fact, there were two communities. The Sephardic Jews came from Portugal and Spain in about 1600 and integrated with the Dutch merchant community. The Ashkenazim came from eastern Europe in 1620 and remained poorer and more isolated. The two communities did not always see eye to eye, but they occupied the same quarter in Amsterdam. Rembrandt had contacts with the Sephardic community. He liked to use Jewish models for his biblical scenes and received help with the Hebrew writing in *The Feast of Belshazzar*.

Marriage

In 1633, Rembrandt met Saskia van Uylenburgh (1612–42), a niece or cousin of Hendrick van Uylenburgh. From an inscription on a drawing Rembrandt made of her in June, it is clear that he was engaged to her then, and the charm of the drawing indicates that he was smitten. Saskia became his model and muse in the years that followed. After they married, they lived with Hendrick van Uylenburgh for about two years before setting up home on their own.

▼ *The Rembrandthuis was big enough to contain a studio for Rembrandt on an upper floor and had more studios for pupils on the top floor.*

1634 Rembrandt marries Saskia van Uylenburgh in Friesland. He becomes a citizen of Amsterdam and a member of the painter's guild, the Guild of St. Luke.

1635 In December, Saskia gives birth to a son, Rumbartus, who dies two months later.

1638 Their second child Cornelia (named after Rembrandt's mother) dies at three weeks.

1640 He suffers two losses: the deaths of a second daughter, also called Cornelia, and his mother.

1641 Titus is born, Rembrandt's only son to survive to adulthood.

Saskia van Uylenburgh

Saskia was six years younger than Rembrandt. She came from a distinguished and wealthy Calvinist family from Friesland, in the north of the Netherlands. Her father had been burgomaster (mayor) of Leeuwarden, the provincial capital, but both her parents had died. Marrying someone of Saskia's rank improved Rembrandt's social status. For their part, the van Uylenburgh family may have been uneasy that Saskia was marrying an artist and the son of a miller, but they appreciated Rembrandt's connections with the Dutch court. However, they soon became concerned that Rembrandt was squandering Saskia's wealth with his extravagant lifestyle.

Rembrandt's House

From 1636, Rembrandt and Saskia lived in rented houses. In 1639, Rembrandt purchased a very grand merchant's house, still called the Rembrandthuis, next to van Uylenburgh's house in Sint Anthonisbreestraat (now Jodenbreestraat). The price was 13,000 guilders, a vast sum for the day. Rembrandt was allowed to pay for the house in installments over several years.

◄ Saskia as Flora *(1634). Rembrandt often painted Saskia in costume. Here she is dressed as the Roman goddess of flowers.*

Children

Families were large in Rembrandt's day. He himself came from a family of nine children. Large families offered some security against the constant presence of death through disease and war. Saskia's first three babies all died within two months, not an uncommon experience for the day. Only her fourth child, Titus, born in 1641, survived to adulthood. Children were nearly always born at home, so Rembrandt was close to the joys and agonies of birth as well as the pain of bereavement, all of which can be detected in his tender drawings of Saskia and her babies.

◄ Saskia with Her First Child Rumbartus *(1635) is a red chalk drawing.*

The painting entitled The Prodigal Son in the ~~t~~vern *(1635) is clearly a self-portrait with Saskia.*

Rembrandt's Studio

Some of Rembrandt's Most Famous Pupils

1628–32 Gerrit Dou (1613–75), Rembrandt's first pupil in his Leiden years, went on to have a distinguished career.

1629–32 Isaac de Jouderville (1613–45) was also a pupil in the Leiden years.

1632 Jacob Backer (1608–51).

1633–7 Govert Flinck (1615–60) became a leading Amsterdam artist.

1635–41 Gerbrand van der Eeckhout (1621–74) became a close friend of Rembrandt.

1635–43 Ferdinand Bol (1616–80) also became a leading Amsterdam artist.

1640–6 Samuel van Hoogstraaten (1627–78).

1641–4 Carel Fabritius (1622–54).

1647–51 Nicolaes Maes (1634–93).

1650–4 Willem Drost (c. 1630–c. 1680).

1661–8 Aert de Gelder (1645–1727), one of Rembrandt's last pupils, was a devoted follower.

From the beginning of Rembrandt's professional career, he took on pupils. He probably had more than forty pupils over his lifetime. Pupils had to pay for the privilege of being taught by a distinguished master, so they provided Rembrandt with an income. In addition, they made a valuable contribution to the work carried out in the master's studio. Rembrandt had a studio when he lived with van Uylenburgh. In 1636, he converted a warehouse on the Bloemgracht into a studio. After 1639, he could accommodate five pupils at his new house at Sint Anthonisbreestraat.

A Painter's Materials

In Rembrandt's day, artists could not simply buy tubes of ready-made oil paint. Instead, they had to obtain raw materials — pigments such as iron oxide, clays, chalk, and soot — and mix them with linseed oil. They painted with oil paint on canvas stretched over a wooden frame and also on wooden panels. They used brushes made of animal hair and also carried a stick with a padded end, called a maulstick, to help steady their hands when working on detail. Rembrandt, like most other artists, wore a robe over his clothing while painting (see page 6).

▲ *A painting dated 1637, possibly by Gerrit Dou, shows an artist in his studio at work on a stretched canvas mounted on an easel.*

▶ *As depicted in this engraving, while the artist stood at his canvas, pupils busied themselves preparing paints and learning the trade.*

Pupils and Assistants

In busy workshops, such as Rembrandt's, it was the job of pupils to prepare the materials for the master — stretching and priming canvases, grinding the pigments, mixing in the oils, and preparing the master's palette with the chosen range of paints. Time was also set aside for their instruction, practicing drawing, learning anatomy and perspective, and studying the work of Old Masters. Some pupils went on to become assistants, helping the master with his teaching tasks and his painting — usually parts of the background or the clothing. Rembrandt also accepted some amateur pupils who were not training to be professional artists but wanted to learn out of interest.

▶ *This* Self-Portrait *(c. 1645) by Gerrit Dou shows many similarities with Rembrandt's self-portrait, in turn inspired by Titian.*

▼ *This version of* The Sacrifice of Isaac *(1635), now in Munich, is a copy with touches by Rembrandt.*

Rembrandt's Followers

Many of Rembrandt's pupils later had successful careers as professional artists, and some, such as Govert Flinck and Ferdinand Bol, became more popular than Rembrandt in their lifetimes. Carel Fabritius was perhaps Rembrandt's most gifted pupil, but he died young in an explosion of a gunpowder storehouse that also destroyed much of his work. Of all the pupils, Gerrit Dou probably has the greatest international reputation today.

▼ *The original version of* The Sacrifice of Isaac, *(1635) is now in St. Petersburg, Russia. In composition, it strongly resembles a work by Rembrandt's teacher Pieter Lastman.*

Attribution Problems

Another of the pupils' tasks was to make exact copies of major works by the master, sometimes many years after the original was painted. At this time, there was no great concern that a painting was entirely by the artist who claimed it or that it was a unique original. If collectors liked a painting, they could ask for a copy to be made, probably from art dealers' studios like van Uylenburgh's. As a result, it is often difficult to be quite sure who painted what. Rembrandt did at least sign most of his work. Like Leonardo da Vinci, Michelangelo (1475–1564), and Titian before him, he wanted to be known only by his first name, which is how we know him today.

The Night Watch

1638 The queen of France, Maria de' Medici, (1573–1642) makes a state visit to Amsterdam.

1640–2 Rembrandt paints *The Night Watch*. An English traveler records that Rembrandt is one of the "excellent men" producing art in the Netherlands.

1642 Rembrandt received payment of an average of 100 guilders from each of the sixteen civic guardsmen in *The Night Watch*. Henrietta Maria (1609–69), former Queen of England and daughter of Maria de' Medici, visits Amsterdam.

1648 Both the Eighty Years' War and the Thirty Years' War come to a close.

Rembrandt was now at the height of his career. In a biography published in 1641, he was described as "one of the most celebrated painters of this century." His contacts and their recommendations provided a ceaseless supply of well-paid commissions. Through one portrait commission, he met the head of the musketeer branch of Amsterdam's civic guard. This connection led to one of Rembrandt's most ambitious and most famous paintings, known as *The Night Watch*.

◀ *By Rembrandt's era, many of the militia guilds had become more like gentlemen's drinking and dining clubs. This drinking horn comes from Amsterdam's Guild of Musketeers.*

Guilds and Corporations

In 1634, Rembrandt joined Amsterdam's Guild of St. Luke, the guild for painters. This was one of many professional guilds in the city, established in the Middle Ages to set trading standards and protect craftsmen and other interest groups. The different branches of the army also had their own guilds, such as the Amsterdam Guild of Musketeers.

Frans Hals

One of the leading Dutch painters of Rembrandt's day was Frans Hals (1582/3–1666). Although he was born in Antwerp, Flanders (in the Spanish Netherlands), his family soon moved to Haarlem, in the United Provinces of the Netherlands, where by tradition, Dutch art is said to have been founded. Hals was the first of the great Dutch portrait painters and an important reference for Rembrandt, especially in his use of free and fluent brushstrokes. He painted not only individual portraits but also the kind of group portrait that was in demand from the militia guilds.

▼ A Banquet of the Officers of the St. George Civic Guard *(1616) by Frans Hals.*

Militia Companies

By the 1640s, although the war with Spain was not yet over, the fighting was mainly taking place abroad or at sea. The role of the militias, or civic guard, had become primarily ceremonial and social, although they had to be ready for action in the event of attack. Frans Banning Cocq, captain of musketeer militia, was a wealthy and ambitious man who also held the title of Lord of Purmerlandt. He wanted a painting of his militia that reflected his status and sense of panache. The original title of the painting was *The Young Heer van Purmerlandt, as Captain, Orders his Lieutenant, the Heer van Vlaerderdingen, to March the Company Out*. It became known as *The Night Watch* only later, when the varnish become badly discolored and made the painting look very dark.

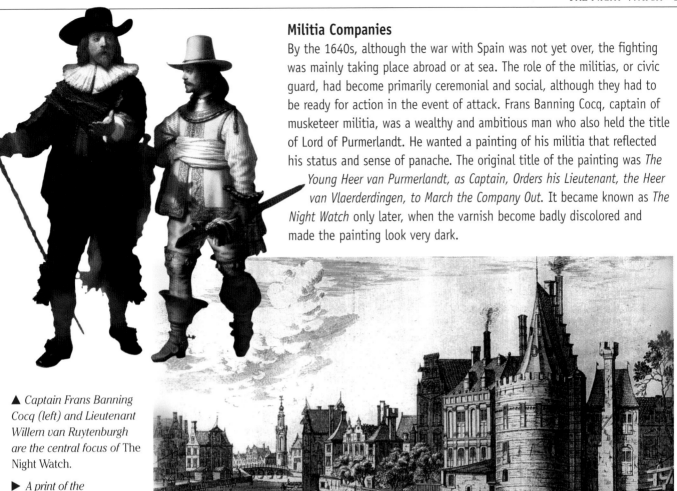

▲ *Captain Frans Banning Cocq (left) and Lieutenant Willem van Ruytenburgh are the central focus of* The Night Watch.

▶ *A print of the Kloveniersdoelen shows the extent of the property, which included a range where the musketeers could practice shooting.*

The Challenge of the Kloveniersdoelen

The Night Watch was made for the new wing of the Kloveniersdoelen, the headquarters of the musketeer branch of the civic guard, which lay close to Rembrandt's house in Nieuwe Doelenstraat. It was to be one of six large group portraits of militia companies (three others were painted by Rembrandt's pupils Govert Flinck and Jacob Backer). This presented Rembrandt with a challenge similar to the one he faced over *The Anatomy Lesson of Dr. Tulp:* he needed to outshine all the others. The traditional approach was to give equal weight to each of the sitters as in Frans Hals' painting of the St. George Civic Guard. Rembrandt felt that this approach made the portrait too static.

▶ *The French artist Jacques Callot (1592–1635), one of the greatest printmakers of the age, made a famous series called* The Miseries of War, *on which this painting was based.*

The Brutality of The Thirty Years' War

While the Eighty Years' War (1568–1648) continued, another even more devastating war was taking place in Germany, called the Thirty Years' War (1618–48). Again, the cause was religion. It began with the revolt of Protestants against their Catholic rulers, the Habsburgs. This drew in the Protestant Danish and then the Swedes. The repeated offensives and counteroffensives laid waste much of Germany and were brought to a close only after France entered the fray against Habsburg Spain. This was a war of almost unprecedented brutality, marked by massacres and starvation; it cost the lives of some five million people. It no doubt reinforced Rembrandt's leanings towards pacifism.

The Night Watch

Dynamic Composition

The Night Watch shows the Militia Company setting out from their headquarters on a mission. That mission remains unclear; it may have been the official reception of Maria de' Medici, the former queen of France, in Amsterdam in 1638. The painting hums with activity. To avoid the usual static quality of traditional group portraits, Rembrandt has given different emphasis to all the background figures, which he was allowed to do because the sixteen subscribers all paid different fees according to the prominence they were given. Originally the painting measured over 14.5 feet (4.5 m) by 16 feet (5 m), but it was trimmed on all sides when it was installed in the Town Hall in 1715, spoiling the balance of the composition.

▼ *The girl, illuminated by light, carries the emblem of the Kloveniers — birds' claws.*

▶ The Night Watch *(1642) was Rembrandt's largest painting; the figures in the foreground are almost life sized.*

1641 After the birth of her son Titus, Saskia falls ill.

1642 Saskia dies on June 14 and is buried at the Oude Kerk (Old Church) in Amsterdam. Geertje Dircx joins Rembrandt's household as a nurse for Titus. Rembrandt finishes work on *The Night Watch*.

1643 He makes his largest and most celebrated landscape etching, *The Three Trees*.

1644 Portrait commissions begin to dry up.

1645 He paints *Girl at the Window*, one of his most popular works.

Death and Landscape

▼ *Saskia with a Red Flower (1641), detail shown here, was painted the year before her death. She holds out a flower, the symbol of fidelity.*

While Rembrandt was engaged with *The Night Watch*, Saskia lay ill at home, and in June 1642, she died. This great personal tragedy occurred just as Rembrandt's fame reached new heights. He could have taken up lucrative commissions to paint society portraits, but instead he appears to have sought solace in landscape, painting, drawing, and etching the scenery that lay outside the city walls. It was the beginning of a change in his approach to art, which now became more exclusively private, personal, and intimate.

Saskia's Death

In the months that followed the birth of Titus, Saskia never recovered her health. Lying at home, weakened and exhausted, it is possible that she contracted tuberculosis, which hurried her toward her grave at the age of just twenty-nine. At the age of thirty-five, Rembrandt was a widower with a baby less than a year old. To help out in the house, he employed Geertje Dircx as a nurse for Titus. She was a country woman about thirty years old. Saskia left 40,000 guilders in her will; before long, her family began to complain that Rembrandt was spending it too extravagantly.

Stormy Weather

During this period, Rembrandt spent more and more of his time making prints using the technique called etching. The black-and-white finish of prints suited his approach to landscape, which was often intensely atmospheric and dramatic. In this respect, he

▲ *The etching* The Three Trees *(1643) shows a gathering rainstorm. It captures a melancholic mood that may have echoed Rembrandt's feelings after the loss of Saskia.*

shows his attraction to the landscape paintings and etchings of the Antwerp school, notably those of Peter Paul Rubens and his friend Hercules Seghers (c. 1589–c. 1638), who often assisted Rubens. Their work showed a delicate balance between drama and naturalism — distant views with gnarled trees and jagged rocks beneath menacing skies. Rembrandt owned eight paintings by Seghers.

Landscape as Subject Matter

Pure landscape painting was a comparatively new pursuit. In the past, landscape appeared as the backdrop to painting, providing the setting in which the main event of the picture took place. Various artists, such as Leonardo da Vinci, had made sketches of pure landscape in the past, but it did not become the sole subject of painting until the seventeenth century. The Dutch in particular made landscape painting a specialty, bringing to it a unique sense of naturalism and honesty.

▶ Winter Landscape *(1623), painted by Esaias van de Velde, was a direct inspiration for Rembrandt's painting of the same name.*

Rural Realism

By 1646, Rembrandt was beginning to take a rather different approach to landscape — finding beauty in ordinary scenes of country life. His inspiration was the artist Esaias van de Velde (c. 1590–1630), who is credited with the introduction of realism in Dutch landscape painting. Van de Velde specialized in small-scale works: rural scenes dotted with a few figures. Rembrandt's work reflects a general trend in Dutch painting that, in contrast to the breathtaking grandeur of Italian-style landscapes, focused on ordinary, contemporary views of the Dutch countryside with cottages, polders, canals, and windmills.

▼ Winter Landscape *(1646) is a small painting measuring just over 6 inches (16 cm) by 9 inches (23 cm). It shows Rembrandt's concern with rendering the Dutch landscape as it was, simple and unglorified.*

c. 1625 Rembrandt begins etching when still in Leiden.

c. 1643–49 He works on *The Hundred Guilder Print.*

1647 He makes three noted etched portraits of his friends: Jan Asselijn (landscape painter), Ephraim Bonus (Jewish doctor) and Jan Six (burgomaster and businessman).

1648 He makes his last etched self-portrait, *Rembrandt Drawing at a Window* (see page 7).

c. 1656 He etches *Abraham Francen, Apothecary.*

1660 Rembrandt abandons etching.

Etching

Rembrandt was one of the most gifted printmakers in the history of art. He pushed forward the evolution of etching and drypoint. He brought a new vitality to etching by drawing more freely on the copper plate than any previous artists had. His fame spread throughout Europe largely through his three hundred or so etchings in circulation. During the 1630s, he worked on several projects to produce large prints, mainly of his own paintings, such as *Descent from the Cross*. After Saskia's death, Rembrandt concentrated on etching and painted less.

▼ *The sharp, V-shaped burin was used in drypoint to scratch lines into the copper plate.*

Copper Plates

With standard etching, a copper plate is first covered in a hard, acid-resistant layer of beeswax mixed with bitumen and resin. The artist then uses a sharp steel needle to draw lines in the wax and expose the copper surface. When the plate is placed in an acid bath, the acid eats into the exposed copper (the lines) but not where the wax remains. The wax is then removed. When ink is applied to the plate, it settles only in the lines, and the image can be printed on paper.

▶ *When printed, the image appears in reverse. Drypoint plates had the disadvantage of wearing out quickly, perhaps after just ten prints were made, while normal acid-etched plates could make up to 250 prints.*

◀ *The copper plate for Rembrandt's* Abraham Entertaining the Angels *(1656) was etched with drypoint.*

Drypoint

Artists can also work directly on the plate, scratching with a sharp, pointed tool called a burin. This technique, called drypoint, was normally used to make adjustments to plates that had already been etched with acid. But Rembrandt often made plates entirely by drypoint. Being able to control the shape and depth of the line by hand pressure increased the sensitivity of the drawing, which was enhanced by the delicate printed effect of the "burr" of metal raised by the burin.

Rembrandt's Artistic Techniques

The process of etching allowed the artist to improve a work in stages by making alterations after each printing. Successive editions made from the same plate were called "states." The originality of Rembrandt's prints is largely due to the variety of techniques he applied to them. He altered the pressure of his etching needle and burin to bring variety to the lines. He mixed etching with drypoint, used varnish to control the effect of the acid, and made corrections with wax and varnish. Also, he used a burnisher to remove lines and strengthen the effect of light penetrating the darkness.

▶ The Artist Drawing from a Model *(c. 1639). The first, sketchy state of this engraving depicts the artist drawing a statue. The startling contrast in light is one of the hallmarks of Rembrandt's prints.*

Subject Matters

Rembrandt applied engraving to an astonishing range of subject matter: copies of his paintings (for promotion), landscapes, portraits, and religious scenes. His greatest project, lasting from about 1643 to 1649, was *Christ Healing the Sick*, which also became known as *The Hundred Guilder Print* because copies sold at this very high price even during Rembrandt's lifetime. Christ, the central focus, appears to be radiating light, an effect achieved by a complex mix of etching techniques. A new tenderness and spirituality appears in Rembrandt's religious work during this period.

▼ *Rembrandt's deep humanity shines through in* The Hundred Guilder Print *(c. 1647), seen here in its fourth state.*

1647 Hendrickje Stoffels joins the household as housekeeper. Prince Frederick Henry dies and is succeeded by his son Prince William II (1626–50).

1648 The Eighty Years' War with Spain comes to a close. The Thirty Years' War also ends with the Treaty of Westphalia, which gives equal status to Protestants and Catholics in Germany; it also marks the decline of Spain.

1649 Geertje Dircx is evicted from Rembrandt's house.

1652 The first Anglo-Dutch War begins.

1653 Amsterdam is hit by plague. Rembrandt is commissioned to paint *Aristotle with a Bust of Homer*.

Home Troubles

During the late 1640s, Rembrandt's promising career began to falter. He was receiving fewer portrait commissions, partly, it appears, because he took a very long time to complete them. Besides, his interests seemed to lie elsewhere — in pursuing the kind of work that pleased him, not flattering the pride of wealthy clients. Meanwhile, his home life was a mess. This was mainly caused by stipulations in Saskia's will. She had left her money to Titus, not to Rembrandt, but Rembrandt had access to it provided he did not remarry. Still leading his extravagant lifestyle, he could not afford to break this stipulation. The result was a very public scandal.

The Anglo-Dutch Trade Wars

The financial climate in Amsterdam had generally taken a turn for the worse, and the situation was aggravated by war with England. The cause of the first Anglo-Dutch War (1652–4) was primarily the English Navigation Act of 1651, which stated that all goods imported into England had to be carried by English ships. The Dutch naval response to these trade restrictions resulted in the blockade of Dutch ports by the English navy until peace, favorable to England, was negotiated. The second Anglo-Dutch War (1665–7) forced the English to amend their trade laws.

▲ *A model of a Dutch fluyt, or flyboat, shows the kind of merchant ship that carried valuable trade goods around the world and in and out of Amsterdam.*

◀ The Holy Family *(1645) may have been inspired by scenes in Rembrandt's household, where Geertje tended to the infant Titus.*

Geertje Dircx

Not long after Geertje Dircx joined Rembrandt's household as nurse to Titus, she became Rembrandt's mistress. Clearly, Rembrandt held out some promise of marriage to her. She meanwhile made a will, leaving all her assets to Titus. This included Saskia's jewelry, which Rembrandt had given to her. But in about 1649, Rembrandt turned his affections to his housekeeper, Hendrickje Stoffels. Geertje, spurned and furious, sued him for breach of promise. She failed, but she did manage to win compensation of 200 guilders a year. She left the house in 1649. Unfortunately, she had meanwhile pawned the jewelry, and when she failed to return it to Rembrandt, he brought a case against her. As a result, she was sentenced to a house of correction in Gouda. She was released in 1655 and died in about 1656.

▶ Rembrandt's Aristotle with a Bust of Homer *(1653) follows a traditional theme that poses questions about art and mortality.*

◀*Rembrandt owned and drew inspiration from busts of classical figures such as Aristotle and Homer (seen here).*

International Reputation

Despite the scandals of his home life, Rembrandt's standing as a painter remained undiminished. His international reputation, spreading largely through his prints, earned him commissions from abroad. *Aristotle with a Bust of Homer*, for instance, was painted for a Sicilian patron, Don Antonio Ruffo. This kind of historical painting was the kind of work Rembrandt preferred to do, but commissions were rare. The result was that he was no longer earning as much as he was spending. Financial pressures began to mount.

Jan Six

In the late 1640s, Rembrandt became friendly with Jan Six (1618–1700), a leading figure in Amsterdam, a former burgomaster who retired from business in 1652 to devote himself to writing. Jan Six was a scholar and a poet. He was also a valued patron who bought several of Rembrandt's paintings. He had an estate outside Amsterdam where Rembrandt was invited to stay and could draw the landscape.

Rembrandt's Social Circles

Rembrandt's many etched portraits indicate his circle of friends — men like Jan Six, the Jewish doctor and writer Ephraim Bonus, the doctor Arnold Tholinx, the artists Roelant Roghman and Jan Asselijn, and the printseller and publisher Clement de Jonghe. Rembrandt thrived in such well-informed and artistic company. This was an era of rationalism with strong emphasis on cultured humanity, all of which is reflected in Rembrandt's work.

▶ *Rembrandt's* Portrait of Jan Six *(1654) shows his increasing tendency to use bold brushwork, which contrasted with the smooth and polished finish offered by most society portrait painters.*

Depicting the Body

1654 Hendrickje is censured by church authorities for immoral behavior. She gives birth to a daughter, Cornelia. Rembrandt paints *Woman Bathing in a Stream*. His *Bathsheba* is a reworking of the Old Testament story in which the sight of the naked Bathsheba induced the envious King David to have her husband killed.

1656 Rembrandt paints *The Anatomy Lesson of Dr. Johan Deyman*.

1658 He makes a series of small etchings of female nudes sitting on a bed.

▼ *Hendrickje almost certainly was the model for* Woman Bathing in a Stream *(1654).*

Rembrandt was a brilliant draftsman, using chalk, silverpoint, and a reed ink pen. Most of his drawings were not studies for paintings so much as works in their own right. His rapid sketches — often of family life or ordinary street scenes — are some of his most effective work, full of charm and spontaneity. His figure work shows a confident grasp of anatomy. Throughout his career, the human body remained the central focus of his work.

▶ Woman Bathing her Feet at a Brook *(1658), one of many Rembrandt etchings on this theme.*

The Nude in Art

Nudes became an important subject in Western art during the Renaissance, in imitation of the nudes in classical sculpture. Rubens' female nudes showed a particular kind of sensuous vitality, which seems to have inspired Rembrandt, who similarly used nudes in many of his scenes of classical myth. It was a subject that he addressed particularly in his etchings, often portraying women at intimate moments of their private lives, such as bathing.

Hendrickje Stoffels

After Rembrandt and Hendrickje became lovers, she appears to have become Rembrandt's new muse and model, in much the same way as Saskia once had been. Their relationship, however, caused problems. In the summer of 1654, she was called before a church council and condemned on charges of immorality for living with Rembrandt in an unmarried state. This seems to have had little impact on either of them. The following October, she gave birth to a daughter, Cornelia (1654). Rembrandt was unable to marry Hendrickje because of the terms of Saskia's will.

▲ An Elephant *(1637). This charcoal sketch shows the ready accuracy of Rembrandt's eye in creating a thoroughly convincing impression of an animal that would not have been very familiar.*

▶ *An illustration of the dissection of the brain, from* De Humani Corporis Fabrica, *shows close similarities with Rembrandt's cadaver.*

The Anatomy Lesson of Dr. Johan Deyman

In 1656, through his doctor friends, Rembrandt received another major commission for a group portrait centering on an anatomy lesson, again for the Amsterdam Guild of Surgeons. This time he placed the eight sitters more conventionally around the surgeon, but the cadaver was shown feet forward and dramatically foreshortened. We can only imagine how the final painting looked because most of it was destroyed in a fire in 1723.

▶ *Only about a quarter of* The Anatomy Lesson of Dr. Johan Deyman *(1656) has survived.*

Animals

Rembrandt also made studies of animals and painted them with convincing realism. Dogs appear in a number of his paintings. In *The Night Watch*, a cowering dog adds to the tension of the scene (see page 25). Another dog appears in his *Self-Portrait in Oriental Costume with a Dog* (see page 40). His understanding of the anatomy of animals is made clear in works like *The Skeleton Rider* (1655), a drawing that shows a human skeleton riding the skeleton of a horse. Other animals that appear in his work include horses, lions, pigs, and chickens.

Vesalius

For anatomical reference, Rembrandt used the famous illustrated work *De Humani Corporis Fabrica* (*On the Construction of the Human Body*) by the Flemish doctor Andreas Vesalius (1514–64). He was physician to Charles V and Philip II of Spain, but while he was at the University of Padua in Italy, he carried out numerous dissections of cadavers. Although *De Humani Corporis Fabrica* was published in 1543, it remained the most complete reference book available. It is fairly certain that Rembrandt used Vesalius's book when depicting the dissected arm in *The Anatomy Lesson of Dr. Tulp* (see page 13). Vesalius became known as the "father of modern anatomy."

Bankruptcy

1653 Rembrandt is forced to borrow nearly 10,000 guilders to pay off the money owed on his house. He borrows a portion of it from Jan Six.

1655 In December, and in January 1656, Rembrandt holds sales of works from his collection to raise money.

1656 Rembrandt applies for voluntary bankruptcy. In September, the first public auction of his assets takes place.

1658 Sales of his assets continue. His house is also sold, and the family moves into rented accommodations on the Rozengracht in the poorer district of Jordaan.

In 1653, in the worsening financial climate of Amsterdam, the owners of Rembrandt's grand house in Sint Anthonisbreestraat demanded the last installment of the purchase price. Rembrandt managed to raise the money, but over the coming years, his debts continued to mount. His income was simply insufficient to fund his debts or match his expenditures. In 1656, he filed for bankruptcy — or rather, he volunteered to hand over all his assets to his creditors. All his possessions were sold at auction.

◀ *This gilded snail made from a nautilus shell is typical of the popular kind of curio that combined natural objects with artistic craftsmanship.*

▲ *A printed bill announced the sale of Rembrandt's collection at the Keizerskroon Inn in September 1658.*

The Inventory

The inventory of Rembrandt's possessions provides a fascinating insight into his world. Carefully listed in 363 lots are many ordinary household items, such as pots and pans and linen sheets. But there was also a huge and impressive collection of art — valuable paintings by great masters such as Raphael, Giorgione (c. 1477–1510), and Jan van Eyck (1395–1441), prints by Pieter Brueghel the Elder (c. 1525–69), Lucas Cranach (1472–1553), and Rubens, as well as a large collection of his own work.

A Passionate Collector

For years, Rembrandt had been spending money extravagantly at auctions and sales, buying prints, paintings, and artistic props such as the weapons and costumes that appear in his paintings. Many wealthy people, including Rembrandt, also collected curios — anything that they found fascinating that could be displayed on shelves and cabinets. These included items such as seashells, medals and coins, porcelain figurines, and Indian artifacts. Such collections were statements of the owners' wide-ranging intellectual curiosity.

A New Business Venture

The Guild of St. Luke prevented bankrupt members from trading. Hendrickje and Titus (then nineteen), reorganized Rembrandt's business in 1660 to try to revive his fortune. They took over ownership of Rembrandt's work and paid him as an employee. This arrangement also protected him from creditors.

◀ *Titus (c. 1658). Early in adulthood, Titus had to shoulder the burden of his father's business and legal affairs.*

The New Town Hall Commission

An unfortunate blow to Rembrandt's self-esteem occurred in the early 1660s. Shortly after peace with Spain was declared in 1648, work began on a new Town Hall (Stadhuis) for Amsterdam. Large-scale paintings were commissioned to decorate the interior, but the commissions went first to Rembrandt's pupils and his old colleague, Jan Lievens. Rembrandt was only asked to contribute when Govert Flinck suddenly died in 1660. The authorities did not like Rembrandt's painting, *The Conspiracy of the Batavians under Claudius Civilis*, and returned it after a few months.

▲ The Conspiracy of the Batavians under Claudius Civilis *(1661) remains only as a fragment; the original was cut down for resale.*

▶ Abraham Francen, Apothecary, *(c. 1656) ranks as one of Rembrandt's finest portrait etchings.*

▼ *The Town Hall, overlooking Dam Square in central Amsterdam, is now the Royal Palace.*

Abraham Francen

Rembrandt's financial distress was not related to any reduction in his standing as an artist. Rather, it was the result of his inability to manage his wealth and his unwillingness to do the kind of portrait work that would bring in an income. He still had a large number of supporters, some of whom helped him financially during bankruptcy proceedings. They included Abraham Francen, an apothecary, art collector, and close family friend. Francen also provided financial guarantees for Titus.

Late Portraits

1661 Rembrandt's Sicilian patron Don Antonio Ruffo commissions two new paintings, *Alexander the Great* and *Homer*, but Ruffo complains about them, and they have to be sent back for amendment.

1662 Rembrandt paints *The Syndics of the Drapers' Guild* and also receives valuable commissions from the wealthy Trip family.

1663 Plague returns to Amsterdam; Hendrickje dies.

1665 Rembrandt paints a portrait of the painter Gerard de Lairesse, whose face is deformed by sickness.

1665–7 The second Anglo-Dutch war causes disruption to trade.

1666 Rembrandt paints a portrait of the poet Jeremias de Decker.

Despite all his setbacks and his growing social isolation, in the early 1660s, Rembrandt threw himself into a new and energetic period of productivity. Now he all but abandoned etching for painting. A boost to his self-confidence came from a new major commission, a group portrait of *The Syndics of the Drapers' Guild* (1662), for which he won great acclaim.

Rembrandt's international status earned him a visit from Cosimo de' Medici III (1642–1723), later the Grand Duke of Tuscany, in 1667.

▼ Portrait of Jeremias de Decker *(1666) is remarkable for the shadow cast by the hat brim, which adds intensity and mystery to the eyes.*

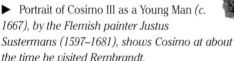

▶ Portrait of Cosimo III as a Young Man *(c. 1667), by the Flemish painter Justus Sustermans (1597–1681), shows Cosimo at about the time he visited Rembrandt.*

Psychological Penetration

Rembrandt's financial difficulties were still causing him distress. He could no longer afford to run a large workshop and ceased taking on new pupils; Aert de Gelder was one of his last. Rembrandt was even forced to sell Saskia's tomb in the Oude Kerk, and he moved her remains to a more modest grave in the Westerkerk. Such hardships seem to have informed his late portraits, which are filled with a deep and riveting sense of human understanding. This is seen, for example, in his *Portrait of Jeremias de Decker*. Decker, a poet and a pupil of Joost van de Vondel (1587–1679), the Netherlands' greatest writer, was a close friend of Rembrandt and maintained loyally that Rembrandt was a better artist than either Raphael or Michelangelo.

Homes of the Wealthy

Virtually all wealthy Dutch families had collections of pictures as well as sculptures and curios. A collection was a way to display a family's status, knowledge, and cultural sensitivities. Some houses included dedicated rooms where the collections were on show. Typically, the walls were covered in paintings several rows deep. Art dealers had similar galleries where collectors came to view the works for sale. In other private houses, paintings were distributed around a series of rooms, often arranged around a courtyard, along with collections of fine furniture, carpets, curios, and musical instruments. Print collections were not usually framed but kept in portfolios on stands, from which they could be removed, examined, and passed around. The overall effect was one of great comfort and material luxury, but on a modest scale, without the showy grandeur of the palaces and stately homes of nobility in other European countries, such as France.

◀ Interior of a Picture Gallery *(1630–5), by the Antwerp-based painter Frans Francken II, shows how paintings covered the walls.*

▼ Portrait of Hendrickje Stoffels *(1654). This portrait is presumed to be of Hendrickje, although she cannot be definitely identified in any portrait.*

▶ Girl with a Pearl Earring *(c. 1665) was painted by Jan Vermeer in the closing years of Rembrandt's life.*

Johannes Vermeer

The painter who remarkably portrayed the interior of seventeenth-century Dutch homes was Johannes (or Jan) Vermeer (1632-75), who worked in the city of Delft. His few paintings (totaling only about forty) are noted for their clarity of detail, their silent contemplative mood, and his ability to capture a fleeting moment. Vermeer is generally considered the second-greatest Dutch artist of the seventeenth century, after Rembrandt.

Hendrickje's Death

In the summer of 1663, Hendrickje suddenly took ill and died, probably one of Amsterdam's nine thousand victims of the bubonic plague that swept through Europe. She was buried in the Westerkerk of Amsterdam. Once again, Rembrandt, at age fifty-seven, found himself alone, with two children, Titus, who was twenty-one, and Cornelia, who was eight.

Late Portraits

▼ *For many critics*, The Syndics of the Drapers' Guild *(1662) is Rembrandt's most satisfactory group portrait. The viewer's eye is drawn to each of the sitters individually, yet they fit together as a unified composition.*

The Syndics of the Drapers' Guild

The Drapers' Guild brought together leaders of the Amsterdam cloth industry. There were five main sitters (with hats), plus the servant placed in the middle to the rear. It is not in fact clear whether they are the syndics (the administrators) or the sampling officials — both titles have been used for the painting. Rembrandt approached the commission in a fairly conventional way, giving each sitter equal weight. Nonetheless, he has injected a touch of spontaneity through the pose of the standing character and the alert expressions. In addition, the viewpoint from beneath the level of the table is refreshingly unusual. The result is sympathetic and harmonious.

The Burgomasters

Each of the cities of the Netherlands, including the Spanish Netherlands, had its own distinct identity and loyalties. The cities governed themselves virtually like independent ministates. They were administered from the town hall by elected officials drawn usually from the merchant classes and the guilds. In charge, and holding office only for a specified number of years, were the burgomasters (masters of the borough), who were roughly equivalent to mayors but with real legal and administrative powers. Amsterdam had a council of four burgomasters who served alongside the other regents who governed the city.

▼ *The office of burgomaster implied wealth and power as well as social pleasures, as seen in this detail from* Supper at the House of Burgomaster Rockox *(1630–5) by Frans Francken II.*

The Cloth Industry

Cloth was the cornerstone of trade in many of the cities of northern Europe. The raw materials — wool and linen — were bought and sold, dyed, woven into bolts of cloth, and made into garments, bed linen, and countless other items of daily need. There were numerous different types of cloth and countless variations in quality. It was the job of the sampling officials of the Drapers' Guild of Amsterdam, who were appointed by the city burgomasters, to monitor the quality of cloth traded in the city and to set industry standards. As witnessed in many of his paintings, Rembrandt took a particular interest in cloth and a special delight in showy, shiny kinds, such as brocade.

◄ *A detail of a painting by Pieter de Hooch (1629-84) that shows many of the ways in which cloth was put to use in a Dutch household.*

Self-Portraits

1625 Rembrandt paints himself in the background of his first dated painting, *The Stoning of St. Stephen.*

1629 *Self-Portrait* (page 9), from his Leiden years, is his first dated self-portrait. He also produces his first etched self-portrait.

1631 Rembrandt paints *Self-Portrait in Oriental Costume with a Dog.*

1648 He etches *Rembrandt Drawing at a Window* (page 7).

1658 He makes his last etched self-portrait.

c. 1661 He paints the famous self-portrait as an artist with semicircles in the background.

1669 Rembrandt paints three self-portraits in the final year of his life, including the "laughing" portrait.

Rembrandt painted at least eighty self-portraits over his lifetime, from the 1620s on. In his early career, he followed an old tradition of using himself as a model for exploring expressions and attitudes — angry, smiling, open-mouthed. He also painted himself in a variety of roles, dressed in various guises. With his bulbous nose and broad, rough features, he was not exactly handsome, but he depicted himself with an appealing honesty. Over the last twenty years of his life, he became brutally frank about his looks. In these late works, a kind of intimate communication, a mutual understanding, hovers between Rembrandt and the viewer, resonating through the silence like a conversation.

▶ *A detail of the self-portrait from page 6, dating from about 1629, shows Rembrandt in his work clothes with his palette and maulstick.*

Early Portraits

Through his self-portraits, it is possible to track Rembrandt's unfolding career and his development as an artist and a person. His early self-portraits contain a youthful vigor, the swagger and self-confidence of a man with talent and ambition. In some paintings, by contrast, he is little more than a clotheshorse wearing a disguise and playing a role for the sake of an exercise. He was, on such occasions, simply the most convenient model at hand. Even here, however, he exhibits his unfailing knack of communicating personality.

▶ His Self-Portrait in Oriental Costume with a Dog *(1631) is one of many early works for which he adopted an exotic disguise.*

With Palette in Hand

Many of the later self-portraits show Rembrandt with disarming honesty in his work clothes, just as he would have looked in the mirror as he painted. By the 1660s, Rembrandt was beleaguered by financial troubles and bereavement, and his face often displays a look of resignation, but there is also a sense of smoldering determination. His rapid, rough brushstrokes transmit a lively, spontaneous immediacy, as if capturing a moment of his life like a snapshot. These paintings were created for his own pleasure and interest; when he applied such roughly-finished techniques to commissioned portraits, the unpolished surface often drew criticism, although some critics understood that the roughness of the surface dissolved magically into harmonious form when viewed from a distance.

▶ *In this* Self-Portrait *(c. 1661), Rembrandt was about fifty-six years old. This is one of his most celebrated self-portraits, noted for the scratches made by the butt end of his brush and the vigor of the paintwork with its rapid brushstrokes. The mysterious semicircles in the background help balance the composition.*

◀ *In this* Self-Portrait *(c. 1669), one of Rembrandt's last, his old face lights up with a cheerful grin.*

▲ *A detail from one of his self-portraits shows how Rembrandt engages the viewer with the eyes.*

Full Circle

One of Rembrandt's most remarkable self-portraits, painted right at the end of his life, shows him in three-quarter view, smirking happily, as ever catching the viewer with his eye contact. Possibly this was his interpretation of the legend of the ancient Greek painter Zeuxis (late fifth century B.C.), who died laughing while painting an ugly old woman. It is strongly reminiscent of another of his self-portraits — his first, painted some forty years earlier (see page 9). Between the two lay a lifetime of experience, which shows in the paintwork as well as in the features. But quite clearly, it is the same person: the same soul looks through those eyes — a testament to Rembrandt's ability to capture the inner nature of the people he painted.

c. 1667 Rembrandt paints *The Jewish Bride*. Titus marries but dies within the year.

c. 1669 He paints *The Return of the Prodigal Son* and *Simeon with the Christ Child in the Temple* plus three self-portraits. In March, Titus's daughter, Titia, Rembrandt's only granddaughter, is born. On October 4, Rembrandt dies.

▼ *British physicist Robert Hooke (1635–1703) designed the microscope in the 1660s.*

The Final Years

Rembrandt cut a lonely figure in his final years. Fashion in art had moved on, favoring ever more polished surfaces and flattering portraiture. His own impatience and irritable temperament had alienated many patrons and clients who might have helped him. He had always been bold and experimental in his painting technique, especially in his more private work. Now his paintwork became even more loose, vibrant and expressive. He was no longer concerned with *chiaroscuro*. His subjects seemed to glow with their own light.

▼ *The Jewish Bride (c. 1667) may possibly be a portrait of Titus and Magdelena — or if not a portrait, then symbolic of them. A remarkable feature of this painting is the shimmering effect of the luxurious clothing rendered in close detail.*

Extending the Power of Sight

During Rembrandt's lifetime, the world of science and learning advanced in leaps and bounds, assisted by tools designed by Dutch spectacle makers that magnified the powers of observation. The microscope is believed to have been invented as early as 1590. The telescope was later invented by Hans Lippershey (c. 1570–c. 1619) in 1608. Also during the seventeenth century, Antonie van Leeuwenhoek (1632–1723) developed lens-grinding techniques that allowed him to view bacteria. It took several decades, however, before improvements began to show the true potential of these inventions.

Titus and Magdalena

In 1668, Rembrandt's son Titus married Magdalena van Loo (1642-69), the daughter of a silversmith who had been a friend to both Rembrandt and Saskia. Titus left the Rembrandt household to live with his wife. Rembrandt was now living alone with his daughter Cornelia, who was fourteen. Just seven months after his marriage, Titus died at the age of twenty-six. He was buried at the Westerkerk. Six months later, Magdalena gave birth to a daughter, Titia. Magdalena died later that same year.

Working to the End

In his final years, Rembrandt lived a very modest life in the Rozengracht house, eating bread and cheese and herring, cared for by his fifteen-year-old daughter and a servant girl. He never ceased to work, even in his old age. By now his brushwork had become much more loose and free. His colors glow gold and red and sparkle with highlights. He painted three self-portraits in the last year of his life — the grinning one and two more stately ones, sitting upright, puffy face half-turned to the viewer, bearing a bemused smile. One of his last works was *Simeon with the Christ Child in the Temple* (1669), which depicts the devout old man who recognized Christ as the Messiah before dying in peace.

▶ *The paintwork is sketchy, but* Simeon with the Christ Child in the Temple *(1669) shows tenderness and emotion.*

▼ *The Westerkerk (Western Church) was built in 1620–31 not far from the center of Amsterdam.*

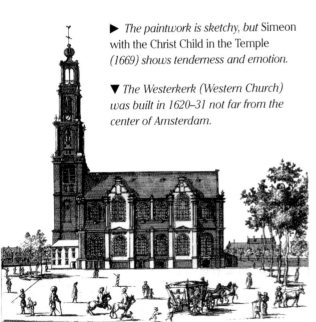

Dutch Still Life Painting

Rembrandt was remarkable for his range of technique and subject matter. Many Dutch artists, by contrast, specialized in just one kind of painting, such as still life painting, which grew in both skill and importance as the seventeenth century progressed. One of the most gifted still life artists was Willem Kalf (1619–93), who settled in Amsterdam in 1453. Outwardly, Dutch still lifes are superbly painted images of domestic items, such as food and tableware, their glinting surfaces reproduced to almost photographic perfection. They are also symbolic on two levels. In general, they represent loving appreciation for the objects portrayed, underlining the value of the kinds of crafted material things with which well-to-do Dutch traders surrounded themselves. In addition, still lifes often contained a host of symbolic messages: a snuffed-out candle, for instance, symbolized death.

◀ Still Life *(1662) by Willem Kalf. Still lifes usually contained a range of luxury goods, including fine porcelain and Turkish rugs.*

Rembrandt's Death

Rembrandt died on October 4, 1669, at the age of sixty-three. His death went virtually unnoticed in Amsterdam. There were no public expressions of mourning as there had been for Pieter Lastman and Govert Flinck. In Antwerp, the whole city had mourned at the death of Rubens. Rembrandt, by contrast, was buried in a simple ceremony in the Westerkerk, in an unmarked pauper's grave somewhere near Hendrickje and Titus. The exact location of his grave is not known. It is probably as Rembrandt would have wanted it. His monument is his art.

Rembrandt's Legacy

1718–21 The Dutch painter and writer Arnold Houbraken (1660–1719) publishes his three-volume *Great Theater of Netherlandish Painters*, the most important source book about seventeenth-century painters.

Early nineteenth century The Romantics revive Rembrandt's reputation.

Mid-nineteenth century Gustave Courbet champions Rembrandt. A renaissance of engraving leads to reappraisal of Rembrandt as one of the great masters of the technique.

1968 The Rembrandt Research Project begins its mammoth task of assessing the authenticity of some six hundred paintings said to be by Rembrandt.

Rembrandt always wanted to be recognized as an outstanding artist, one of the great masters. Today, this is indeed how he is viewed. But he has not always had this reputation. His significant international reputation at the time of his death proved precarious. In the seventeenth and eighteenth centuries, his painting was criticized for its "unfinished" look, and a certain vulgarity was detected in his subject matter. His portraits were not sufficiently grand and flattering. It was only in the nineteenth century that his work began to be fully appreciated for its technical innovation and for his uncompromising stance as an artist who put his own artistic integrity before commercial gain.

▼ *A detail from* Liberty Leading the People *(1830) is typical of the emotionally-charged paintings of Eugène Delacroix.*

Courbet's Realism

One of France's most gifted and controversial painters of the nineteenth century was Gustave Courbet (1819–77). He liked to call himself a "Realist," painting the world as it was without prettifying it or interpreting it. Courbet recognized a similar approach in Rembrandt's work, not only in his landscapes but in paintings such as *Woman Bathing in a Stream* (see page 32). He felt that Rembrandt painted what he saw with honesty and candor — not glorified or beautified but simply selected and revealed in its natural, unpretentious charm.

Delacroix's Admiration

Earlier in the nineteenth century, the painters in the French Romantic movement, such as Eugène Delacroix (1798-1863), championed Rembrandt because they felt that he had suffered for his art. They developed an exaggerated image of him as an old man, forgotten and misunderstood but risking his reputation for truth in art and self-expression. Rembrandt's use of rapid, energetic brushstrokes appealed to them as a way of conveying passion. The Romantics effectively salvaged Rembrandt's reputation, and from that point on, his work became increasingly admired and increasingly valuable.

◄ The Man with a Pipe *(c. 1846), a self-portrait by Gustave Courbet, shows a concern to convey spontaneity and character.*

A Master's Hand

Each generation sees something new in the work of the Old Masters. When the Impressionists began to paint in a rapid, sketchy style to capture the moment and mood of a landscape, they looked at Rembrandt's late work and saw how he had achieved much the same effect. In the 1870s, when Impressionism was new, many critics complained that their work looked "unfinished." This was precisely the same criticism leveled at Rembrandt. Indeed, when his house was cleared after his death, a notary found thirteen "unfinished" paintings — which included *The Return of the Prodigal Son* and *Simeon with the Christ Child in the Temple.* Today, we would not be so quick to judge.

▶ *A detail of* The Return of the Prodigal Son *(c. 1669) shows the emotional power that could be transmitted by the rapid brushstrokes of Rembrandt's later work.*

Attribution Problems

Telling true Rembrandts from copies or works by his pupils has remained a thorny problem. Not all Rembrandts are clearly signed, and in any case, a signature is not a guarantee of authenticity. Complex analysis has to be carried out before any work by Rembrandt can be declared genuine. This has been the task of the Rembrandt Research Project, which since 1968 has been sorting out the true Rembrandts from the doubtful ones.

◀ *"Rembrandt van Rijn"is how he signed a document dated 1665. He also signed his paintings.*

Where to Find Rembrandt

The paintings of some artists look as good when printed in a book as they do in real life. This is not the case with Rembrandt's. The surface quality of his paintings — the rough brushstrokes, the dabs of thick impasto, the scratchings — are an integral part of the overall effect and reveal his craftsmanship. The good news is that there are Rembrandt paintings in major public galleries all over the world: in Boston, New York, Chicago, London, Cologne, Hamburg, Paris, Lyon, and St. Petersburg. The best place to go is the Dutch national gallery, the Rijksmuseum, in Amsterdam.

◀ The Night Watch, *exhibited in the Gallery of Honor in the Rijksmuseum in Amsterdam, attracts art lovers from around the world.*

Glossary

abstract A style of art that does not represent objects as they appear in reality but reduces and simplifies forms and objects. Abstract art abandons the traditional principle that art must imitate nature.

anatomy The study of the organization of the body in separate parts.

attribute To credit an artist with the creation of a work of art.

authenticity The genuineness or legitimacy of something.

bankruptcy Complete inability to pay one's debts.

burin A tool with a sharp point used by an etcher or engraver to carve lines onto the surface of a wooden block or metal sheet.

burr The thin ridge of metal raised above the surface of the metal plate created by a burin or graving tool. In drypoint engraving, the burr collects ink and produces a soft, rich line on the engraving. Only a limited number of prints can be obtained this way because the burr is ultimately crushed during the printing process.

Calvinist A person who follows the teaching of John Calvin (1509–64), a Christian reformer who formed a new branch of Christianity that emphasizes the complete power of God over people's fate or destiny.

chiaroscuro An Italian term meaning "lightdark" that describes an effect used in art, showing the contrast between light and shade.

classical Term used to describe works of art from ancient Greece or Rome, or works that have the same characteristics as the works of ancient Greece or Rome.

commission The act of appointing someone to do a specific task, or the actual task given to someone under an agreement, especially in terms of creating a work of art.

composition The arrangement of the parts of something. The term is used to refer to the way in which objects are arranged, usually in a painting or sculpture.

Counter-Reformation The movement of the Catholic Church against the Protestant Reformation in the sixteenth to early seventeenth centuries that sought to strengthen the Catholic Church.

draftsman A person who is skilled in the art of drawing.

drypoint A method of engraving in which a needle or sharp tool is used directly on the surface of a metal plate to create a design without the use of acid. The burr created by the carving of the metal surface with the tool produces particular effects in the finished product. Drypoint is often used to make additions to an etching.

etching A method of engraving in which a design is burned onto a metal plate using acid, or the print taken from the process.

foreshortening Creating the illusion of extension of an object in space by depicting it in proper perspective and proportionately shortening the side pointing directly toward the viewer.

guild An association representing a trade or craft in medieval and Renaissance Europe.

humanism A cultural movement of the fifteenth century based on the study of classical texts, or a system of thought concerned with the needs of people rather than with those of religion.

impasto A technique used in painting in which layers of paint are laid on the canvas, usually thickly enough that the brush or painting knife strokes can be seen. Paint is usually mixed right on the canvas.

Impressionism A nineteenth-century art movement that took a more spontaneous approach to painting, attempting to capture and portray the atmosphere of a given moment, usually identified by a strong concern for the changing qualities of light.

iron oxide A substance made by the combination of iron and oxygen. Iron oxide has varying colors, usually reddish-brown or blackish-orange, and is used as a pigment.

linseed oil A yellowish, drying oil made from flaxseed that is mixed with a pigment to make oil paint.

maulstick A long stick used by a painter to support his or her hand while applying paint.

Mennonite A member of the Christian church founded by Menno Simons (1496–1561) that believes in full authority of the Scripture.

muse A person who inspires an artist's work.

Old Master An artist of an earlier period, usually from the fifteenth to the eighteenth centuries, of noteworthy skill.

patron A person who gives money to a person or group to perform a certain task or for some other worthy purpose. Patrons sometimes support artists and writers.

perspective The method of representing objects so as to make them appear three-dimensional. The illusion of depth and space or a view extending far into the distance.

pigment Any substance, usually in the form of a fine powder, used as a coloring agent to make paint. A paint or dye.

polder An area of land, once covered in water, that has been drained and is used for farming and pasture. Polders are commonly found in the Netherlands.

Protestant A member of any Christian Church or community that separated itself from the Catholic Church during the Reformation.

realism In art, a movement that started in France in the mid-nineteenth century, the aim of which was to create accurate representations of reality.

Remonstrants The Dutch followers of Jacobus Arminius (1560–1609) who, refusing to accept all of the doctrines of Calvinism, formed their own sect in 1610.

state A stage in the engraving or etching process, or the various editions made from the same plate, usually with alterations.

still life A painting in which the subject is a group of inanimate objects. Still lifes first appeared in the sixteenth century and became popular in Flanders and Holland after the Reformation when religious scenes were no longer in demand.

triptych A painting composed of three parts or panels.

Index

Albert, archduke of Spain 14
Amalia van Solms, princess of
    Orange 12
Amsterdam 6, 8, 9, 10, 12, 13, 17, 18,
    22, 23, 24, 26, 30, 31, 34, 35, 36, 37,
    38, 39, 43, 45
    Dam Square 12, 35
    Jewish quarter 17
    Jordaan district 34
    Oude Kerk 26, 36
    Rembrandthuis 6, 18
    Rijksmuseum 45
    Royal Palace 35
    Rozengracht 34, 43
    Sint Anthonisbreestraat
        (Jodenbreestraat) 6, 18, 34
    Town Hall 24, 35
    Westerkerk 36, 37, 42, 43
Anglo-Dutch Wars 30, 36
Antwerp 14, 22, 43
Asselijn, Jan 28, 31

Backer, Jacob 20, 23
Banning Cocq, Frans 23
Belgium 8
Bol, Ferdinand 20, 21
Bonus, Ephraim 28, 31
Brueghel, Pieter 34

Callot, Jacques 23
    Miseries of War, The 23
Calvin, John 16
Calvinists 16
Caravaggio 10, 11
    Calling of St. Matthew, The 11
Charles I, King of England 10, 14
Charles V, King of Spain 33
Christ 17, 29, 43
Cosimo de' Medici III, Grand duke of
    Tuscany 36
Counter-Reformation 14
Courbet, Gustave 44
    Man with a Pipe 44
Cranach the Elder, Lucas 34

Danish (people) 23
de Decker, Jeremias 36
de Gelder, Aert 20, 36
de Hooch, Pieter 7, 39
de Houtman, Cornelis 12
de Keyser, Thomas 11

de Jonghe, Clement 31
de Lairesse, Gerard 36
Delacroix, Eugène 44
    Liberty Leading the People 44
Dircx, Geertje 6, 26, 30
Dou, Gerrit 10, 20, 21
    Self-Portrait 21
Drost, Willem 20
Dutch East India Company 12
Dutch West India Company 12

Eighty Years' War 8, 22, 23, 30
England 14, 30
English Navigation Act of 1651 30
Europe 10, 14, 17, 28, 37

Fabritius, Carel 20, 21
Far East 12
Flanders 22
Flinck, Govert 20, 21, 23, 35, 43
France 14, 23, 24, 44
Francen, Abraham 35
Francken II, Frans 37, 39
    Interior of a Picture Gallery 37
    Supper at the House of
        Burgomaster Rockox 39
Frederick Henry, prince of Orange 7,
    11, 16, 30
Friesland 6, 18

Germany 23, 30
Giorgione 34
guilds 22
    Drapers' Guild 38, 39
    Guild of Musketeers 22
    Guild of St. Luke 18, 22, 34
    Guild of Surgeons 13, 33

Haarlem 22
Hague, The 6, 11, 12
Hals, Frans 22, 23
    Banquet of the Officers of the St.
        George Civic Guard, A 22
Habsburgs 23
Henrietta Maria, Queen of England
    22
Houbraken, Arnold 44
    Great Theater of Netherlandish
        Painters 44
Huygens, Constantijn 10, 11, 13, 16
Huygens, Maurits 13

Isabella, Infanta of Spain 14
Italy 11, 33

Jews
    Ashkenazic 17
    Sephardic 17
Jouderville, Isaac 10, 20
    Constantijn Huygens and his
        Clerk 11

Kalf, Willem 43
    Still Life 43

Lastman, Pieter 6, 8, 9, 10, 11, 12,
    17, 43
    Balaam's Ass and the Angel 9
Leeuwarden 18
Leiden 6, 7, 10
    University of 8
Leonardo da Vinci 10, 16, 21, 27
    Last Supper, The 16
Lievens, Jan 8, 10, 11, 35
    Portrait of Rembrandt 11
Lippershey, Hans 42
Lopez, Alfonso 15

Maes, Nicolaes 20
Maria de' Medici, Queen of France
    22, 24
Michelangelo 21, 36
Middle Ages 12, 22
Mierevelt, Michiel 16

Netherlands (United Provinces
    of the Netherlands) 6, 7, 8, 9, 11,
    16, 18, 22, 36, 39

Padua, University of 33
Philip II, King of Spain 8, 33
Philip IV, King of Spain 14
Portugal 17

Raphael 14, 15, 34, 36
    Portrait of Baldassare Castiglione
        14, 15
Rembrandt Harmenszoon van Rijn
    drawings
        Elephant, An 33
        Saskia with her first Child
            Rumbartus 18
        Skeleton Rider, The 33

Index

etchings
  Abraham Entertaining the
    Angels 28
  Abraham Francen, Apothecary
    28, 35
  Artist Drawing from a Model,
    The 29
  Christ Healing the Sick see
    Hundred Guilder Print, The
  Hundred Guilder Print, The
    (Christ Healing the Sick) 28, 29
  Rembrandt Drawing at a
    Window 7, 28, 40
  Three Trees, The 26
  Woman Bathing her Feet at a
    Brook 32
paintings
  Abduction of Ganymede, The
    14, 15
  Alexander the Great 36
  Anatomy Lesson of Dr. Johan
    Deyman, The 32, 33
  Anatomy Lesson of Dr. Tulp, The
    6, 12, 13, 23
  Aristotle with a Bust of Homer
    30, 31
  Balaam's Ass and the Angel 9, 10
  Bathsheba 32
  Conspiracy of the Batavians
    under Claudius Civilis, The 35
  Descent from the Cross 14, 28
  Feast of Belshazzar, The 17
  Girl at the Window 26
  Holy Family 30
  Homer 36
  Jacob Blessing the Children of
    Joseph 7
  Jewish Bride, The 42
  Last Supper, The 16
  Night Watch, The 6, 22, 23, 24, 26,
    33, 45
  Portrait of Hendrickje Stoffels 37
  Portrait of Jan Six 31
  Portrait of Jeremias de Decker 36
  Portrait of Maurits Huygens 13
  Presentation of Jesus in the
    Temple, The 10
  Raising of the Cross 14
  Return of the Prodigal Son, The
    42, 45
  Sacrifice of Isaac, The 21

Saskia as Flora 18
Saskia with a Red Flower 26
Simeon with the Christ Child in
    the Temple 42, 43, 45
Stoning of St. Stephen,
    The 6, 7, 40
Syndics of the Drapers' Guild, The
    6, 36, 38
Titus 34
Winter Landscape 27
Woman Bathing in a Stream
    32, 44
self-portraits
  Artist in his Studio 6
  Prodigal Son in the Tavern,
    The 10
  Rembrandt Drawing at a
    Window 7
  Self-Portrait (1629) 9, 40
  Self-Portrait (1661–62) 41
  Self-Portrait (1669) 41
  Self-Portrait at the Age of 34 15
  Self-Portrait in Oriental Costume
    with a Dog 33, 40
Rembrandthuis 6, 18
Roghman, Roelant 31
Rubens, Peter Paul 14, 15, 26, 32,
    34, 43
  Descent from the Cross 14
  Judgment of Paris, The 14
  Raising of the Cross 14
  Self-Portrait 14
Ruffo, Don Antonio 31, 36
Ruts, Nicholaes 12

Seghers, Hercules 26
Six, Jan 28, 31, 34
Spain 6, 7, 14, 17, 23, 23, 30, 35
Spanish Netherlands 6, 8, 14, 22, 39
St. Petersburg 45
Stoffels, Hendrickje 6, 30, 32, 34, 36,
    37, 43
Sustermans, Justus 36
  Portrait of Cosimo III as a Young
    Man 36
Swedes 23

Thirty Years' War 22, 23, 30
Tholinx, Arnold 31
Tintoretto 10
Titian 7, 10, 15

Portrait of a Man 15
Treaty of Westphalia 30
Trip family 36
Tuscany 36
Twelve Year Truce, The 8

Union of Utrecht 16
United Provinces of the Netherlands
    (Dutch Republic), see also
    Netherlands, 8, 10, 22

van der Eeckhout, Gerbrand 20
van Eyck, Jan 34
van Honthorst, Gerrit 11
van Hoogstraaten, Samuel 20
van Leeuwenhoek, Antonie 42
van Loo, Magdalena 42
van Rijn
  Cornelia (died 1638) 18
  Cornelia (died 1640) 18
  Cornelia 6, 32, 37
  Harmen Gerritszoon 8
  Rembrandt Harmenszoon, see
    Rembrandt
  Rumbartus 18
  Titia 42
  Titus 6, 18, 26, 30, 34, 35, 37, 42, 43
van Ruytenburgh, Lieutenant Willem
    23
van Suijttbroeck, Cornelia (Neeltje) 8
van Swanenburgh, Jacop Isaacszoon
    8, 9
van Uylenburgh
  Hendrick 10, 12, 13, 16, 18, 20, 21
  Saskia 6, 18, 26, 28, 30, 32, 42
Velde, Esaias van de 27
  Winter Landscape 27
Venice 15
Vermeer, Johannes (Jan) 37
  Girl with a Pearl Earring 37
Vesalius, Andreas 33
  De Humani Corporis Fabrica 33

William, prince of Orange 8
William II, prince of Orange 30

Zeus 15
Zeuxis 41